everyday courage

A COLLECTION OF POEMS

CENTERLIGHT MEDIA
AUSTIN, TEXAS

First Edition, CenterLight Media, August 2022
Copyright ©2022 by Christia Madacsi Hoffman

Cover photography © Christia Madacsi Hoffman,
with thanks to the Adler-Gevurtz family
Cover design by Christia Madacsi Hoffman, CenterLight Media

For permissions or more information about CenterLight Media,
visit CenterLightMedia.com.

Printed in the United States of America

ISBN (original paperback): 978-0-578-28985-4
Also available as an ebook.

CONTENTS

DEDICATION

To my daughter, T,
whose creative spirit I know to be boundless.

ACKNOWLEDGMENTS

For those who dream and do, I am grateful.

For your support, friendship and inspiration, thank you
Elisabeth von Halem; Sarah Warner; Poet Jim Trainer;
Taylor Hoffman; Christine Wyatt; Clay Hoffman;
Filmmaker Andy Cockrum; Filmmaker Tom Procida;
Poet Joe Brundidge; Poet Aimée Mackovic; Dennis Adler,
David Gevurtz and William Bear; David, Karen and
Max Madacsi; Artist and Father David Madacsi;
Wordsmith and Mom, Patricia Bauer; Georgia Ridenhour;
Cheline Jaidar; Telepathist Ralph Sutton;
Artist and Author Elena Hiatt Houlihan

everyday
courage

HOW MANY?

How many have loved you in their way?
Whose minds you've filled, unwitting,
with what could be? Inspired with hope,
energy, reason, all the while, unknowing?
For whom have you been wonderful
and wild? For whom were the glancing blows
of first and late impression softly bruising,
welcome for the rush and flow of blood,
truth and evidence of living?
On whom have you left traces of your being
while becoming yourself?

EVERYDAY COURAGE

It's a good thing doors both open and close,
that locks can be picked, hinges removed,
that grease or two simple tools
can help a handle turn with ease
because I don't intend to wait
for some unseen hand to help,
to let the air and light back in,
if I can open the door for myself

HOW DO YOU KNOW?

In the classroom, she asked plainly,
"How do you know what to write?"
It's like asking about living.
A perennial question about purpose,
conviction. How can you know
which direction to take?
There's no compass for that.
But I wanted to offer something.
Because at seven, we hope
someone will tell us the answers
when we need them and keep
their mouth shut when we don't.
So the answer came back:
"Look around. Listen. See
what invites your attention.
You'll find your way to begin."

LEARN(ING) TO SHARE

Stop being so selfish.
Don't keep it to yourself, he said.
The words in your head might be
the very words someone needs to hear.
Vulnerable? Hell, he said, I'm scared
every time, because you can't know
how words will land when you let them
out, how they'll flow away from you.
But let them go, he said. Share.
There's someone who doesn't know
how to say what they need to.
Someone who needs to hear you.
Yes, you. Forget the fear, he said.
Stop being so selfish.

LEGACY

We already know what it looks like for you to stall,
to consistently half-do, use modesty as cover,
call on a dog-eared history of diffidence, in-habituation,
until we've grown weary of the story, weary of listening.
Instead, what we want, what we're asking,
is for you to speak out, tell us what you've lived for.
Better still, by your medium of choice,
show us how to live, through your thought,
your sight, your voice, else silence persists.
The difference between indolence and self-doubt
is indeterminate, when both leave things undone.
The question is this: Who are you?
Who are you not to leave a legacy?

THIS EARLY HOUR

It used to feel like stealing
– this early hour –
taken from obligation
to family and house
Though now, when interrupted,
I feel the theft myself
of thought, of wandering,
before the day's concerns
come to table, to desk
Even shy of rest
there's nothing I like
quite as well as to be alone
in the eastern light
with wren as my alarm
and reminder
to tightly guard,
whether stolen or by right,
the time I've made mine

SILENT ALCHEMY

This stillness is home-made
It took rising before dawn
and a cup of deep black coffee
a waking blend of habit and drive
that takes one less glass of wine
mixed with added sleep
like wild yeast left overnight
a starter reserved
for the silent alchemy of art

NEED, LOVE, WANT

At forty-eight, I'm learning
to use my words
This arose as a result first
of learning to laugh
not that I didn't know how
just that I wouldn't let it out
For years
didn't think I should take up
so much aural space
laughter is loud sometimes
sometimes wrongly placed
The difference now
is how I let it release,
like the words
need, love, want,
which often turn letters
into what I forever thought
was fate
but that just now,
at forty-eight, I'm learning
finally to form, to speak, to state

LIMITED EDITION

I've been watching of late
how the etchings of age
charged with the ink of years
have darkened in line, how
the paper of skin, bared to sun,
has begun to patina
and I've seen how the descent
of brow matches the days
it took for the scribe to incise
a smile, plate the portrait,
and how, in the gallery of fate,
each is a limited edition of one

SEPARATION & REPAIR

In the space between veneer
and solid wood
the glue sometimes gives
separation occurs
It's usually from time and wear
but sometimes
from neglect, dry air,
or overuse
It takes the right tool –
a honed chisel – to pry it loose,
scrape away the dessicated scale of glue,
a steady hand, a clamp, and patience
to finish the repair
And while the craftsman
will always see the alteration,
a difference in light and hue,
evidence of skilled imperfection,
the restoration will go unnoticed,
so long as the surface holds

RECONSIDER

Let's call it a rose
and for the sake of tradition
– we'll make use of the trope –
a red rose, not crimson, even,
but a brighter tint,
shallow as a promise,
chosen not for its beauty
but because as a signifier
it says love and apology at once,
an admission that one of us
is not worth quite enough
to spend on original thought
Easy enough to pluck up
for the occasion, even more,
believed multiplied in meaning
with each stem
When all along,
the voluminous ranunculus,
the ruffled peony,
fragrant gardenia, buds of freesia,
were nearby, waiting
to share their scent, beauty,
ready to be given, breathed in
With what colors! Subtle blushes
and complex, uncertain shades,
the fairer cousins to red
and reasons enough
to reconsider the rose

RESOLUTION

systems previously separate
come together of a sudden
what could be a clash of concerns
instead elicit harmonies
not fixed or written
but in agreement with
the oscillation that governs
the repetitive variation of
the human heart
predator-prey populations
vibrations of a stringed instrument
from equilibrium
they move by the play of weight and tension
the restoring force of gravity
to build momentum, create heat
store potential in memory
and resolve into a new state

LASTING IMPRESSION

It's a sometimes condition,
an excitable mental cascade
of ineffectual regret following
frustrated expression, steaming
hot at the center, cold at the edges
The unpredictable, uneven oscillation
of mood, circumstance, nature,
invisible radiation moving
too hot, too fast, to control,
once released, contrition can't help,
can't reverse the untold effect
of conduction, words absorbed,
inextricable, to mistakenly become
part of the person you love

coronaverse

THIS DREAM

I share this dream
we'll one day say farewell,
gather at the funeral pyre of hate,
engage fire's power to purify,
recall how it once was, unimaginable,
a pandemic of misdeeds, mistrust,
no mask can cover, safe-keep,
and in the orange glow, see the other
newly cast as we raise our eyes up,
genuflect as one to watch the embers,
the ash, rise and become the air
we breathe, together, inscribe
the headstone deep for generations
ahead to learn yet never know

UNDERWEAR

All my underwear are broken
It's a sign of the times
Crotch liners flapping
like a torn flag, backend elastic
given up, fabric lagging
with each bend and twist
They sag at the waist,
but it seems strange
to throw them in the bin,
having worn them so long
Undies are underrated
We may have our favorites,
but we don't talk about them,
like the jeans that fit
just so, soft and supple, right-
sized and worn in, the pair
we wear with pride
I just can't bring myself
to shop online, place an order,
without touching the lace,
assessing color and stretch
in person for my person
I'm sure I'm not alone in this,
and it may be just a "ladies" issue,
but all my underwear are broken
You? Yes??

INSTRUCTIONS

Instructions for Serendipitous Conversation:
Turn off your phone. Close your laptop lid.
Empty your pockets save for: front door key.
Use the bathroom. Wash your hands.
(You'll need these later.)
Engage with the mirror. Practice your smile.
Pretend you've been asked a question.
Nod. Say, "Yes, and..." This is improvisation,
after all. Check your hair. Your teeth.
Grab a jacket. Umbrella. Whatever
suits the weather. Exit your front door.

Do not give in to the temptation to carry:
phone, earbuds, poor mood. Leave sunglasses
at home. Look out. Do not look down.
Drop your shoulders. Locate the sidewalk.
Step one foot in front of the other. Swing your arms
in the way nature intended. Watch for motion.
If you see a rose in bloom, bend at the waist,
inhale. Take your time. This is not exercise.
This is what we call "a walk." You can also use:
perambulation, constitutional, stroll.
Use your peripheral vision to notice others.
You may be surprised to discover
you're not alone.

PANDEMONIUM

Monday respite, mid-pandemonium,
for those who can afford the rest,
a stay of reality, before we redeploy.
Parents who made lunches make
new lists, unfamiliar: link schedules,
logins, learning objectives; while others
secure masks, cross their fingers,
wait for the bus and the time
we'll round the post- era, the later,
that must finally be drawing close
as butterflies and wildflowers
in the window turn to jack-o'-lanterns
snowflakes, product of hope made
manifest. Each new word mastered,
sum solved, will be evidence of our capacity
to overcome what was too damn hard,
and how pain of frustration, force of will,
proves out the benefit of resolve.

PASS GO

Around the board again.
They'd gladly skip a turn
for a break, to sit still,
watch, wait at a distance.
Better yet, sleep through
until the end, when
after all, no one's really won.
Instead, it's doubles. Roll
another round. Chin up.
In this match, options
are off their table,
with each new shift, duty
dictates reason for return,
and for the rest of us,
the restraint to stay in.

With great gratitude for essential workers.

MORNING, INTERRUPTED

Morning, interrupted
as the night has been,
sign of the times
Even in the in-between,
little space for one full breath
unrestrained by thought,
interruption from duty
Even before dawn,
incursions into sleep
drive out rest,
steer the mind
to territory too familiar,
once relegated to day
Just as the 24-hour news cycle
has neither start nor end,
so, too, when removed
from sun, wind, soil,
thoughts spin
until one horned owl,
Bewick's wren, a battle of jays,
deploy distraction
to penetrate the line
and entice the will to play

AS SLEEP RETIRES

Sleep draws down her hood,
lays her mantle across my bed,
fragrant with night air, starlight.
From my dream state, I stir with
the added weight and heat, shift
shoulders, hips. Seek the cool
underside of feather, cheek
refreshed, set with new conviction
that it's not over yet. One leg
now extended, the other tucked,
feet undressed in desperate
attempt to stay under, protected.
But she considers it done, falls in
beside me, stretches wide
until I have no more claim
to sheet, to rest. And so
resigned I rise, as sleep retires.

RESTRAINT

Even from here

with space between

I know you, know

we'll fill back in

the open time

the unmade, undone

later, make more

for having made do

if for now we share

a common patience

and each convene

in our restraint

TIME TO GO OUT

The quiet of the early days is done,
roadways awake again, crossed and rerun
by necessity, errand, the need to not
stay in, to follow urge beyond the door,
leave the pent-up uncertainty for
solid pavement laid with the knowledge
that we move, keep moving, whether
it ever made sense, only now, we're
aware of the difference, how it pulls
from the silence, overcomes thought,
morning's rest, a feeling in the blood,
like a dog who waits, knowing it must
by now be time, time to go out

RE-TURNING

When we sit back up, eyes open
wide enough to see consolation
won't be ours anytime soon,
not in the way we had dreamed,
anyway, the thoughtful re-turning
of the key, free of the silt
of worry, clean of guilt for grace
Won't have the satisfaction
of certainty, even then, when
we resume, re-assume our post,
the hopeful position, won't know
if we might prefer the morning
before the forward churn begins
again, the new normal overturned
once more, we might lie back down,
and close our eyes just to listen
to the comfort of our own breath

FIRST SOURDOUGH

It's no wonder the French
think their bakers essential
closest incarnation to creator
prove dough and our potential
worth the effort to rise
If only to breathe in the scent
of country boule, crisp baguette
born of conditions varied
in attention, fermentation, fire
and tested by our yearning
for more

PROXIMATE CONNECTION

As of now, 7.8 billion people
populate the Earth, each
subject to imperfect incarnation:
Beyond sustenance, shelter,
we arrive with a need for touch,
for proximate connection closer
than six feet. We name asterisms
known only to us, formed
by virtue of incident, interest,
and a desire to place ourselves
one among and from another.
In distance now we ask
serendipity to wait, absent
the warmth of a kiss, give us
time to redefine fate within space
and know the relief of embrace.

EVEN AS THE DOVE

Blame it on the wind, yesterday,
that rocked the trees, gave reason
to look skyward, see the wren, jay,
chickadee, each on wing to remind
us of the stretch of liberty
we'll earn with each sun, yet,
with watching came a jump
in the rhythm of my blood,
an impulse to join them, to know
again the sense of suddenness
that alerts the mind, adrenaline,
to the unforeseen, unpredictable,
what amounts to experience
Even now, with the wind again low,
I feel land-locked, restless,
and wonder how to be even
as the dove, adjust to the sway,
and remember to stay open within

IN PLACE

It's been awhile since I boarded a plane
without agenda, without a plan in place
on the other end of commercial smiles,
foil-wrapped cheeses, seat-back amusements,
the momentary panic of a misplaced passport,
pleasantries and plastic exchanges,
made in an effort to both lose and find myself

These days, I'm learning how to fly in place,
navigating turbulent take-offs and landings
through practical lessons in patience,
through packing and repacking emotions,
learning a new language of expectations
that feels foreign and native at once,
in an effort to stay grounded and to let go

ARC OF DAYS

wren never has waited on the sun
but pulls her thread of song
through the gray arc of days
spools it from fence to tree
not to warn or censure
but to certify the tilt and turning
of earth toward star
and to reassure us
there is reason still to sing

HIGHER GROUND

Wet with tears whose force
could shame a hurricane
she squeezed dry her fears
and hung them on the line of faith

poured water from a bottle
to wash her cheeks of salt
the fresh taste of despair
from her throat

fatigued beyond thought
she could only watch
as the room flooded with resolve
and the suddenness of safety hit

finally overcome
she drifted on a wave of sleep
carried by the sounds of refuge
to the higher ground of hope

TEST RUN

one test can turn the mind
test the edges of imagination
cause thoughts to curl back, recoil,
as if touched by flame
flee to safety, to warmth without fire,
without pain of waiting
until results result in exhalation
and the future rushes in
to close the wound of unknowing
when the limits of time again blur
with indistinction
when she can get on with living

STILL CHANGING

In situ, but moved from within
different than we might have been
a mere three hundred and sixty five
days before we knew
how to adjust
without shifting weight
to find direction without turning
how to dance in place
With so much the same
it might look as if
we've been waiting
for some outside force or weight
to impact our balance
arrange for displacement
while all year we've been learning
understanding is its own
form of change

SILENT DISSONANCE

questions rise and fall
the in- and exhalation
of eloquent breath
a backdrop of evenings
spent without recompense
to sleep or reason
the spoken word preferred
to the written, then,
when history can be heard
in the particular phonation
and placement of the tongue
with one regret only
of where to land
following the crescendo
and how to resolve
the silent dissonance
in leaving

ELLIPSIS

Words despair for want of reason
uncertain, letters assemble
shift, sort, reorder
run long, run short
spell reaction, spell fact
fail to clear the confusion
Ellipsis sees its moment,
it's used to doubt,
used to waiting,
wordlessly, it steps up
full with meaning,
ready now to stand in,
to stand for understanding
. . .

everyday courage

civic
lessons

HANDS, UNFOLDED

Hands unfolded, he said,
I want you to live
with your hands unfolded
As if he told of a time, a state,
he could see him grow, his son,
without the need to shield
his face, set his jaw,
against a coming of age
A time where the persistence
of lines, laws, drawn down
the center of centuries,
of cities, gridded for greed,
could no longer predict
the statistics of fate
And he could grow, his son,
unimpeded, walk, run, sleep,
breathe, easy, arms at his side,
hands, unfolded

GERRYMANDERED

How to remove, replace,
what practice of years, dictates,
set down, redrew, fenced out,
fenced in, marked as evidence,
yellow-taped, wound in, wound up
into county lines, city streets,
rap sheets generations long
removed from the instance
of hubris that first compelled
one man to press another
to his will, against grounds
long tilled with inequity.
When equal has never been,
there is no choice to reinstate,
only the necessity to draw down,
rebuild, recast the foundation
of rights, inviolate, and the sight
of justice, duly served.

INDIVISIBLE

the scent of fires burning yet
recalls voices, distanced now by night,
now fallen silent as the sound
of the uptick, invisible and gathering,
waiting for an in, indivisible
by profession to party, agnostic
to belief, while down the road,
across the state, loads rise, keep pace
with the July heat, strain patience,
with the yearning to ease discomfort
of days spent restrained, restricted
by collective malaise, our intolerance
for a foe equipped to flout the freedom
to choose, elect, whether we care
for one or another in the name
of country and the spirit
of independence

ELECTION DAY

At the flywheel of fate,
we collect desires and hopes,
only the slightest pressure required
to depress enter, next,
an electronic slate, invisible
to the eyes of the monitors,
and blind to color, class, faith
Just for now,
each stands, individual,
at the same awkward angle,
spinning one single finger,
separate but equal,
in the exercise of will

INHERENT IMBALANCE

Even with the advances of age
we don't forget
what we were taught to accept
as evidence of our worth and place
Asked to pay twice
for advantage taken
attentions ignored
offense withstood
Tasked with raising the bar
we'll rise to the occasion
to test the bias of power
with timorous voice
that strengthens our resolve
to hear each other out
So that sooner we might transcend
the inherent imbalance
and any need to remember
or appeal to believe

MAN, SUPREME

Each morning
he snaps his bias at his waist
pulls up his authority
tucks in his agenda
zips and buttons his beliefs

takes a sip of coffee
before he buckles his conviction
ties rhetoric at his neck
shines his shoes of sin

takes a bite of toast
washes doctrine on his chin
brushes faith onto his tongue
sets opinion in his grin

slips into his pockets
forged tokens of concern
to pay the toll of office
and false gravitas of men

BORDERED DREAM

In his tongue he carries
archives of a country,
a hidden history that requires
friendship to divulge

Among the stout tents, wired fence,
a shared dipthong
separates them both
from the sounds of home
but together gives shy hope

All the while
he's not allowed to cry,
let plosives pile up against
his lips for *papá*, spill
murmurs for *mamá*

civic lessons

He's been told not to hug or touch,
at the risk of scolding,
permitted only to recall
a comforting embrace

Lines up for daily chores,
for lessons in civics and language
that don't yet belong to him
and on the phone he'll confirm
he's brave and strong

If his love survives intact
it will be our turn to dream,
to hope, he might also learn
to be forgiving

ONE THIN BOARD

Another arrest, another revelation,
outside, a hurricane cycle of transgressions,
updated by the hour, replayed across devices
While indoors,
it's not as if there's no swirl of wind,
a microcosm of the broader conditions
Disagreements, tears,
pressurized frustrations
that corrupt the idyll,
like the unsustainable walls of fear,
erected in the name of nation,
faith, security
Choose your affiliation and you'll find
reasons to stay inside,
justification to secure a policy
of protectionism
like a bolt on the door
While in reality, there's just one thin board
between safety and violation

civic lessons

Whether you're in or out,
shifts of identity occur over time,
just as we to learn to clean our room,
practice patience, consideration,
hold all-hands discussions,
resolve our differences in the interest
of evolution and the whole
One day again, we'll have to open up,
welcome change at our doorstep,
to gain perspective and to grow

ELECTION DAY

Up in the air, no clear winning sweep
of the broom, hammer and nail in wood,
last rights read, chapter closed
I wanted to hear the bell toll for good
They've now said get used to the division:
opponents we may be, but not enemies
I'm not so sure how to take that
when the competition's goal is to dismantle
the very system that permits us to speak,
show our opposition to the prevailing rule
When self-interest takes the shape
of munitions, strips rights for restrictions,
I'm left to wonder

AMERICAN DREAMER

On stage, the arc of hope
behind him, he stood poised,
prepared with lecture and elocution
made smooth by trial and inheritance
From his position at the lectern,
he deployed the tools of rhetoric
to show again how intellect and humor
are the better friends of civics
How in history only recently made,
there's cause to attend the social good
and an etiquette for change

GOOD & MAD

Good and Mad, she called it,
a recent volume and recounting
of critical action, stark reminder
of what I've elected to forget
or ignore about social constructions,
about race, about war
So much wisdom, fury of the ages,
now resting at my bedside,
paused between pages,
where it seems I've selected
as bookmark a sheet torn
from a gummed pad inscribed
"Things to Do," followed by
nine open lines, as if
I'm meant to fill them in,
make a list, time to reinvest
efforts made by rages past,
lest their energy be squandered,
take a turn to change the outcome
before she pens the epilogue
It happens that this very day,
a call was made, an address,
which suggests it's for us now
to resolve, advance the cause,
even if he left us out,
or especially because
So while the list for redress
is endless, I'll begin with this.

HUMILITY

I'm just gonna guess
you missed the lessons on hubris.
In case you want the recap,
according to your religion,
it's a sin. Deadly, in fact.
You may want to know
your physician can't help here,
but that book you held up,
that one in the square
that props you up still,
it speaks of the symptoms
and tells of the cure.
It's not new, experimental,
which I know you'd prefer,
but yours alone to administer,
so it's worth taking note:
If you reject the remedy
and your scripture bears out,
you'll be judged at your end
and held to account.

VELVET ROPE

It's hard not to feel rage,
the hot boil of disgust, disdain,
and wonder at the remedy
than can heal a lying nature,
one that spits in the face of reason
and cares only for itself
While he'll contest and disclaim,
the bed he now lies in was self-made
and it's hard to wish for recovery
of an evil that aims to divide us
while he receives the treatment
he's denied those across the table,
the aisle, the flip side of the velvet rope
In his America, if you can buy it,
you get what you deserve

TRUMPED

Innuendo is open
to interpretation, this for that,
believe me,
I give you, my best
effort, if you will, trust
me, let's show them
how business gets done
as long as it's mine
it's good for both sides
how beautiful, people,
millions, make you strong,
you'll see, winning,
it's great again for me,
tremendous,
the best you've ever seen

1989

We carried our Christmas tree
through the streets of Budapest
Stood it straight in the center
of 100,000 former parishioners
of the state
newly released by the fall
In Heroes' Square we lit candles
in celebration of the hammer
that took the first brick,
of the rusting of the sickle
And by the Danube, at parliament,
a red steel star
was wrenched from the sky,
token of a false god,
disseminated like host
among the people
Even at sixteen, an atheist, I knew
the way between was better
than the extremes on either end
Caught a glimpse of both
repression and revolt in action
Now in this new era,
when fear threatens freedom
I put my faith in our collective wisdom
and the ecumenical answer

OPTION COMMAND CONTROL

like a game of chance
I have two options
two commands
but only one shot at control
these backlit keys remind me
of the influence of letters
any sequence might result
in a destiny changed [shift]
life lost or gained [return]
even nuclear threat [delete]
option command control

SPECIAL ORDER

Can I order a friend?
please make it a recurring service
With all that we have on-demand –
movies, books, vegetables, soap –
I figure a person should be easy
Please ship them in
from beyond my five-mile radius
(I work from home;
I could use some outside stimulation)
and by all means,
leave out the notification
of when to expect a knock on the door
I'd rather be surprised,
like when I find my personal shopper
chose the very best peaches
(Though that's pretend.
I still buy my own groceries.)

Really, I'd prefer the imposition
of an unplanned visit
to remind me how it used to be
before Uber, scooter litter, the interwebs
When we would drop in on one another
and welcome the interruption
when home phones rang
until they were answered
and the doorbell sounded
for something unexpected

AT THE POST

In this fine mesh of culture
we find ourselves entwined in a net
we cannot see
caught and newly banded
sorted and recorded by sex,
species, residence, habit

we thought we'd be free
to relate and connect
instead we feed from the post
and with each moment spent
aim to convince ourselves
we are still wild, beautiful,
and sane

TAXES

there is pressure
between the numbers
days of effort brought together
under phantom title
and elusive end
projects, tasks, approvals
hours spent with disregard
for perfect weather
an exchange of days
for dollars
each its own potential
and only one replenishable
once withdrawn
the other, limited to a lifetime
or less
left off the formal ledger
but accounted for later
in resignation, regret
or the conditional tense

STRANGERS

About those we don't know,
Gladwell finds we default
to truth, that unless we learn
otherwise, we assume demeanor
reflects thought, most of us
taught people who appear nice,
or not, have actions to match
We want to believe our eyes
can see and reflect more than
the systems we've received
But when met with evidence
that says otherwise, we discredit
the source, place our own
incredulity first, before those
who would try to have their say,
use as filter what we believe
is proof to the contrary, while we
appeal to the makeshift veracity
of personal history, especially
when the accused pull rank,
and especially when they don't
For justice to have its day,
we have to reflect and reassess,
dismantle years of plan, of practice,
rescind the power to arrest change
and find means to a new right

home

AFTER BASTILLE DAY

Who left the yellow blooms
wrapped in fleur de lys
paper crisp still and clean
rustling in the push and hush
of steps leading to the street
crowded with concerns
all but one
indifferent to the silent gesture
of abandoned intent

home

ALMOST REMEMBERED

I woke with words on my tongue
thick near the surface of thought,
stuck yet to the uncertain state
of dreaming, soft and indeterminate
Sun rising, warm and full as bread,
made it clear it was time, told
of when to drop the hem of sleep
But the words stayed in bed, tucked
beneath all chance of being caught,
where no scolding could recall them
Only a sense of texture remained,
crumb of memory, nearly tasted

THE KITCHEN

Karen comes for breakfast
a basket full of eggs across her arm,
hens' morning gift,
sealed in bloom, still, and stuck with straw
In the sink, we soak them clean,
then break them open,
crack the shells of absence,
pour coffee, add cream,
stir curds of conversation
and Sunday sounds of women
and the kitchen smells of home

SUNDAY TRADITION

Dad measures flour, sours milk with vinegar,
adds salt, baking powder, soda, sugar
mixes egg, butter
pours batter into matching cast iron pans

She makes her approach,
takes her place, spatula in hand,
set for competition:
Whose will be cooked through without burning?
She's learned to keep the heat low
trained her eye, hunger, patience,
tamed anticipation in favor of gold,
in favor of winning

At the table,
they discuss the benefits of height,
spring, crisp edges
she's generous with syrup and praise
But by virtue of post and position,
he says hers always taste best

PAMPLEMOUSSE

In winter, we'd unpack the fruit
each globe wrapped in stiff tissue
showed white, yellow, rose gold
suns of December
My grandmother would slice them through
section and sprinkle them with sugar
as if to make the days sweeter
bright with pink pulp
remedy the ripe sorrows of youth
and the recent scars of age

home

MORAL STORE

Last night, tucked in bed with the Marches,
as cozy in their home in my head as
in my own, sheaves of paper dropping by
like the neighbors, knocking on the door
of memory, like hearing my grandmother,
her moral store of kindness, politesse,
as I recall her, ambassador of manners
and an era when discourse mattered more
than the coarse grain of material wealth
I'm grateful for the reminder of what
she and Alcott taught through daily chore
and character arc: beauty is internal,
humility useful, and humor essential
to grace

ANITA'S LABYRINTH

Morning spreads
brilliant as an eye feather
across the ridge
warms the roof
and lights the rise
she'll later climb
to wind the route of thought
smudge her mind
with air and stone and earth
release what cannot serve
and on returning
she'll find the light without
has shifted
the creek still running
and the light within
renewed

SEPTEMBER WITH CHELINE

We took the route that took
the afternoon to walk, not the one
we planned ahead to take, instead,
the route that gave us time to talk
beside the late-fruiting fig above
the creek, where events of recent weeks
had space to turn, to spread, to rise
beyond the bank and bed of average
times, days the Farmer's Almanac
could not foretell nor we begin to measure,
save by open air, shared affection
and the perspective of September

BLUEGRASS

In her belly, she keeps summers
of bluegrass and barn swallows,
worn-through afternoons,
the rush of charging horseback
and shadow fires at the shore
She keeps the twist for plucking
snap peas, picking bush beans,
the tricky stick shift,
a taste for sun tea, boxed cake,
and soft-serve from town
It's not memory, but knowing,
like how she knows
her sister from a distance,
the sound of the family pickup,
and which turns to take
to make her way home

KENTUCKY LAKE

Hulls sit idle, slip-side, wait for the load:
bait, tackle, patience, petrol,
rods chosen for performance
and the weight of expectation.
Each season, a new cast at play:
diehards, weekenders, dailies,
enthusiasts, all, of unscripted hours
and keepers of fresh mythologies
The reel recalls the lure of living
lakeside, where even in the absence
of success, each is in possession
of a fortune in time

HOUSE SLIPPERS

The shuffle of morning slippers
is my own,
though the cadence I recall
from Father in the kitchen
making coffee downstairs,
unaware of being overheard.
Or Gram, scuffling on pine floors,
dusting her way to salvation,
partly deaf in her left ear.
She could use a toothbrush
and baking soda
to clean anything.
Seems I've inherited a preference
for black joe and a tidy home,
and I've worn through the toe
of my morning slippers.

THANKSGIVING

Post-feast,
there are parties on the streets,
pairs and threesomes,
whose feet aren't familiar
with the unexpected dips and rises,
the fence lines that hide a surprised
dog on day watch
Unaccustomed as they are
to each other, to being closed in
with only shining silverware
and tv for diversion,
they take a walk for air,
the yearly constitutional
that will diminish with age,
as pavements heave,
present new obstacles
to shifting hips, calcified opinions
Until the rituals change altogether,
and they're the ones who stay behind,
cleaning up, while those only now
learning the family secrets,
the favored recipes for living,
grow apart, grow serious,
retire their backyard play
and make their own traditions

MISSING PIECES

Always known my memory
with missing pieces, relied on
yellow album pages to Connect
Four into recollection
Unlike my brother, who stored it
all, drawers full of action figures,
remembrances: the time
I tried to ride his Big Trak,
peeked into the pages of
Am I Normal?, that scene
from Star Wars; seems I need
reminding, yet, I don't forget
the omissions: the Easy-Bake
Oven, Barbie Dreamhouse,
shoes for senior prom;
the budget didn't stretch
that far, but then, tv was free,
and with the river at my feet,
it never occurred to me
we had less or more than another
And if the details don't come
readily, the feeling does:
a wistful sense of youth
and a place called home

ROUTINE

In each house, separate, we drink coffee
Reference school, work, weather
nothing too heavy at breakfast
save politics for dinner

With five feet from beam to fence line
we won't see the sunrise
that would remind us of days passing
Gather lunch, bags, office sweater

Convene at the front door
remember what we left behind
Give hugs, kisses, good day wishes
window wave reflecting light, sky

On the highway of routine
our only exits are illness, mishap, repair
unless we pause to map our way
and choose where we're heading

AGAIN HOME

Back porch light left burning
cat long ago come by the whistle
he alone knows as comfort
scarce needs reminding
what with the cold, the rainfall
the rest of us ignorant
to his imprinted call
the instinctive map tacked
with the same navigational pins
that daily draw women, drive men
down to city's center until
day's dismissal into night
when routed by heart
they return again home

GOOD DOG

On the flip side of the closed door,
he never hesitates, swings it wide
with force, walks through
with the pride of purpose
He's found what he's looking for,
his one charge and duty:
to guard the bed, the floor,
legs of the chair, anywhere
he finds me
He's ready, alert, when I stand,
prepared to move his herd
of one to new pasture, eyes
of blue quartz searching
for answers he never questions
He'll never know why we move
from room to room, why
I sit and stare ahead for hours
What prompts me to suddenly rise,
crash down on him with praise,
wishing to spend the rest of the day
as he does, present as the air

BUTTERS

He sleeps on the landing
in the afternoons
exactly where we need to step
Tan coat camouflaged with carpet
He's trained us to expect him
and the near-miss
of an unplanned trip down the stairs
When it happens,
he yawns and stretches
like nothing in the world is ever new
Slow-rolls to standing,
and jittery with youth,
charges at the dust,
challenges reflections,
at the window, takes issue with the wren
Like so many of his kind,
he's spare with his affection
until it's time to eat,
and with supplicant cries
earns our praise and full attention

SELECTIVE MEMORY

memory, selective,
travels home and back
trimmed in ric rac and cord
passes the threshold
of comfort warmly lit
by filaments of custom
retold, now re-stitched
to a fresh tradition
that fastens past to a vision
of what's newly to come

DIVINE GUIDANCE

I know divine guidance isn't hiding
in the bottom of this coffee cup
It doesn't stop me from looking
each afternoon, within the thin layer
of grounds drained from the stovetop
moka pot that more often than not
expresses beyond intended bounds,
eliciting expletives and a bitter brew
we accept so as not to waste
the labor of the seed picker, roaster,
teamster, grocer, every bean counted
en route to my midday desk
where, even if the hand of fate
isn't stirring yet, ready to redirect,
I'll drink up anyway and wait

WINTER PEACHES

Some days, I can't bear the organic peaches
just out of reach
bright pyramids of privilege
in the VIP produce section
I want them no matter the season
to select from the dusted heads tilted just so
to show their rosy blush, their pinkest cheek

Sometimes I turn them over, as if considering
there's sense in four ninety-nine a pound in winter
as if there's satisfaction to be found
in the hard snap of flesh
summer reserved for a reason
If I breathe deeply enough,
I may catch the bouquet
find one honest, ripe fruit
Maybe this one is worth it

KITCHEN DRAWER

I afix each silence with meaning
pulled from the kitchen drawer of my mind
the one jumbled with odds and ends:
the spare Allen wrench, size unmarked,
phantom keys to decommissioned locks,
twist ties, Velcro dots, dull pencils,
Sharpies that only sometimes work
Why keep these thoughts in circulation?
Isolated, silence is neutral and weightless,
but when the tradition of call-and-response
becomes a one-way conversation
I fumble through my catch-all of speculation
when instead I could use the stateless quiet
to sort what time and age have taught

austin

TRAIL RUNNING

Bent at the waist
in hip-high prairie grass
he needed only sight and
the recent work of rain
to unearth what a century
of soil had covered
The trails of the escarpment
since retread, rewired,
but where the Apache,
Comanche, Tonkawa lived,
they left clues in the Balcones,
never guessing what fault
would divide them,
knap them like flint
from their source stones,
reroute the river
and bury their stories
alongside their fate

HEAT WAVE

Finally broken, the string of days
that run so hot as to cripple thought.
Morning opens with high clouds
hiding blue, seed no longer straining
for relief of rain, soil soaked through,
sated for the time being. Afternoon,
canvas umbrellas will bloom red,
green, white across porches, invite
repose without retreat indoors.
Shorter day, shifting light, recalls
summer's mature age, nearly over,
and the gift of September, new.

IN CARE OF: THE WEATHER DEPT.

Dear Weather Gods,
We're writing to tell you we believe you may have skipped a season.
With all that's going on, it's understandable
that here and there you might lose track of the fact
that Fall should follow Summer – but it IS the usual cycle.

This year, however, Winter seems to have come on prematurely.
And we thought you should know that, next to Spring,
Fall in the northern hemisphere
is one of the most beloved times of year – and this error
hasn't gone unnoticed. To wit, we're VERY MUCH put out.

There's something else amiss, too.
You've forgotten to supply the western United States
with ample water. And while we're on the issue,
please add warming seas to your list of repairs and corrections.
(We think it has something to do with that ozone layer,
which we realize you STILL haven't fixed. Please advise
if we need to address this concern with another department.)

We understand we may have inadvertently
caused the damage, but we believe this would fall under average
condition and use, or whatever that clause is in our lease
that says we can use this place as we see fit.
And this COULD be covered by our renter's insurance,
but we can't find the policy to save our lives. (We'll keep looking.)

Signed,
Your Humble Servants,
Humankind

SUMMER-READY

Beyond the window, I see how
the live oak expects this early sky
Undresses in shadow,
tries on pink first, then yellow,
calls her consort dove
and invites the wren to rise
while the worm drapes her in silks
and moss adorns her umbral crown
She is rooted deep, ready for the season
when the dew dries from the ground,
when blue keeps its southern promise
to hold the sun clear of cloud,
turn lightly tinted morning to white noon,
as summer duly arrives

MORNING'S STAGE

Just shy of August and day's heat clings
through morning, curfew suspended, when
twilight, who knows the rules of the season,
lingers, shows her purple hues to the west,
pinks to the east, before she takes her leave,
gives dawn the stage to do as she pleases,
as the house lights come up, flood white,
and we rise to our feet in reflexive applause

BEFORE THE RAIN

They say the sage blooms
just before the rain
I've noticed she does the same
effuses into flower
litters the ground with lavender
then abstains, pulls her buds in again
in another season
an unsuspecting traveler
would think her plain, simple even,
a sure hedge just for shade or screen
unless he happened by just then
just before the rain

GUN BARREL CYPRESS

Bald cypress stands erect, green yet
in late summer, blue-hued cones
ripening, holding fast their store
for fall, when they'll open, just
as the needles shift, redden to release,
nestle round the protuberant roots
Already, at the water's edge, red ants
make short work of the early drifters,
nuts tumbled open, meat laid bare,
promise of a forest spent and resin
scent's reminder of seasons ahead

everyday courage

opening

BLOOMING

We speak of beauty as if it's static
But its evolution is as captivating
as its pinnacle state
Just as a flower contains the whole of a season
in its bloom, from sprout to stem,
the unfurling, the effort of opening out
to fullest expression,
followed by singular petals loosening,
losing their grip,
or the whole of it,
whorl, stamen, carpel, intact,
taken in an unexpected wind
To nature, we would never say
it wasn't worth it
to attempt her finest hue, a singular scent,
Where would we be if she chose
to give it up, knowing
some of her buds may fail to flourish
or measure up to a flawless ideal

TATTOO

Experience, an invisible tattoo,
like the sand dollar's nautilus track
washed clear from the beach,
once known, takes effect,
like shadow on a sheet,
shifts existence
Just as laughter leaves no trace
yet alters chemistry,
as the singular strings of the cello
in concert reveal a strength of tone,
when bowed by hands that know
how to hold the warmth of weight
that lets her sing

HOW TO BEND

What is it that draws us,
one to another?
Either in friendship
or as lovers,
it's a curious thing.
We move in
and out of feeling,
like wind beneath a branch
causes it to sway
until the bough returns
to a state of rest,
seemingly the same
but different for having moved,
having felt the high of lift
and the opposing dive.
Without the current of air,
without breath,
where would we be?
Would our limbs calcify,
joints tighten, like a mind
taught with stress,
unable to shift?
Perhaps the purpose
is to test our strength
and teach us how to bend.

opening

BEGINNER'S MIND

The scientist said expertise
makes you less likely to think creatively
That is, all that you've learned confines
your ability to conceive of solutions
beyond what you know, unless or until
you cross-train into discomfort,
maintain a mindset that reminds you
there's more to learn, other ways
to perceive, as from a beginner's mind

Think back, she said, to when you began,
when foreign and new were familiar,
and you were assigned mostly to listen
Over time, we find certainty through experience,
but studies show we grow in confidence,
build trust, by taking risks
Instead of leaning on learned beliefs,
our greatest inner innovations arise
through expertise in vulnerability

ARCH CAPE

The stream doesn't ask
to set aside sand,
cast away stone
Instead, she runs as she will
through the lichen and fern,
carries spawn in her eddies,
fish in her currents,
as she clears a new track
by the path of the elk,
den of the fox
Until she falls from the hill
to where the shore
meets her strength,
where her voice,
singular and soft,
greets the chorus of waves,
where she learns of the tide
and joins the depth of the sea

BLOOD MOON

This aubade, by the light of the full moon
that was just last night caught in our umbra
bruised through refraction, for an hour
turned blood red, an occasion to spare sleep,
let wonder ignite possibility, wake the senses,
remind us there is more than what
we might seek to control,
to be touched by the frequency
of red, orange, gold,
as it finds the eye, speeds the pulse,
to suggest fate may have a place
and the Universe a plan of her own

THE ACUPUNCTURIST

Years of practice sit pressed
between jars of inscrutable roots and powders
arranged by frequency of use
Without looking, his fingers know which
contain the formula to lessen pain,
curb obsession, give relief,
and once-foreign words find easy articulation
on a now familiar tongue
From text to training and back again,
each pin placed marks a point of proof,
knowledge of blood and body,
the power of tradition and instinct, both,
in the ability to heal

ADLER'S EYE

Uncommon. Each piece collected with intention.
An assemblage of taste, of interest, vocation.
Evidence of his eye, his attention given
over time, burnished to see beauty
in imperfection
Like the work itself,
I wish it were possible to share
in sight informed by study, by place, reflection.
By knowing firsthand how graphite paced
over paper, leather fastened, pattern woven,
how beam supports floor supports person,
that these when joined, placed with concern,
given full consideration,
form the frame of culture.
I'm grateful he chose, or was himself chosen,
to direct his purpose, apportion talent and intellect,
toward the creation of joy.

NO FORMULA

Color needs light for us to know it,
each shade a wavelength of its own.
Just as velocity and friction describe a stroke:
an equation of bristles,
viscosity of paint,
weight of muscle and skin,
medium meeting medium.

But what of its formation?
Was it the maker's education,
experience, choice,
to strike canvas with brush just so?
Or was it emotion, an unconscious impetus?
Did she know what she wanted?
Or did forces unseen, like ultraviolet and infrared,
like god and love, affect her vision?
We'll never really know.

Luckily for us, creation has no formula,
nor inspiration, proof.

COME ASKING

Noticing
we're due for clouds again
door open, breathing
in the spring air, listening
for the hush beyond,
at this hour, expecting
absence of song, boughs
just now shifting
and within, cat gone,
balm of coffee
on my tongue
Noticing how continuity
is tricky, wears an air
of permanence when
we don't listen
Look closely
to find what was still is now
in motion, light shifting,
birds awoken, cat
come asking for breakfast,
coffee cool and nearly empty
So I'll shift in reply,
mutable after all

WAITING

She waits in unfamiliar light
waits to find what spell might
break open the afternoon
find its way into the living room
with its rich velvet couch
its cerulean porcelain
burnished sterling tea set
crystal laid for six
She sits in foreign solitude
curious to see how it fits her

Even the twin floor clocks
proud in their respective corners
have stopped ticking
made the case for silence
But she's uncertain of her alliance
with the outcome
finds she can't now discern
if she's designed her own confinement
or set herself free

IMPOSTER-POTENTIAL

What's the benefit of an outlook
that falsifies, encodes half-truths, outright
lies about our aptitudes, self-worth
It seems esteem should be innate,
a nature-state we dwell in, when
instead, diffidence, internal friction,
overrides promise, foments self-criticism,
that works its way from the inside out
Over time, builds the walls
of me, myself, and I, installs
a window of belief that contains
vision, narrows sight to limitations
that we convince ourselves are real
How might the landscape look
if instead we build from self-regard
and look out on our potential?

TRAINER

I've noticed
you're not shy of life,
no matter how you brood
I've seen you
swim in the sun,
tickle Jo in your arms,
take up room with song
And I wonder why
it's not enough to keep
you steady on, why
chemistry seems intent
to spoil the mood,
strip glint from your eye,
flatline
In this, you're not alone
I've read
sleep has its effect
and food, no doubt,
blue light, an isolation
all its own
Perhaps it's true,
our cells but a collective
and we, born only to obey
But if capacity is proof,
joy is ours, both,
to know and to permit

BOOK CLUB

In the round, under a quarter moon,
they break words open like bread at table
gather reflections to the center,
turn them over gently with regard,
one for another
Until year over year,
through the language of others,
they reveal stories of their own
and write a new one, together

RESTITUTION

Underfoot, where I once assumed
only dirt, stone and root to exist
I know are fragments
of human experience that won't
resolve themselves into the soil
It's been only a century hence
since clever Hyatt replaced ivory
with a new eight ball
and Leo's Bakelite proved worthy
of a thousand uses for as many years
Yet I've always preferred
the beauty of wood, metal, bone,
having never seen the hues and sheen
of polymer improve in the sun
like mother of pearl, bleached horn

opening

Still, I've been wondering
at how nature adapts to catastrophe,
creates her own, in fact,
and the conditions for change
Given a plastic tree,
if Siddhartha would still counsel us
to detach, train to limit despair
for what's irrevocably lost
It's curious our minds are nimble enough
to replace cost with hope,
and in the soot of our own making,
engage the possibilities
in restitution and repair

INOSCULATION

In horticulture, coaxing two
limbs together, inosculation,
requires more than proximity
It takes the wearing away
of the outer bark, inner phloem,
to reach the cambium,
the very cells responsible
for differentiation, one tree
from another, and for growth
Exposed, they fuse, conjoin,
with time, bark forms again,
seals a new union as if
it always were, a natural fit,
that even with fact, explanation,
leaves us to wonder at chance

EMOTIONAL ADVANCE

What if we applied the same expectations
of our intellect to our emotions?
Could we advance our ability to feel?
As a species, are there feelings we've never
expressed? Undiscovered beneath the
surface of mouth and brow, muscles
made for something else? It would be
the find of the century, to discover
a sentiment that combined the chemistry
of the amygdala, insula, hypothalamus,
to express a response yet unknown.
How would we even explain it?
Its existence like the element in the core
of an accelerator, detected for an instant
and impossible to store, save as memory
and potential. With each of us, then,
participants in the search for more.

taylor

XI7

her bike stands upside down,
pedals up, wheels free to spin
she's been riding in the sky
I'd like to try that
dream of a new force
after years of reigning in,
restricting possibility to perception
through equal parts reason
and imagination, it's the art
of those who write the laws
to test and change them
I'll then source my inspiration
from the laboratory of youth
to begin again to dream

NEVER HAS BEEN

"There never has been a tomorrow,"
she said with the certainty of sages
brought up through the age of man
She's right, of course,
the mythology of time dispersed
across days yet to come —
a secret pocket,
a cup that can't be filled
or drunk from —
is as false as the tongue of the teller
who fills each sunrise with promises
If anything, you'd think we'd perceive
that tomorrow is as fabled as yesterday
if it goes unused, arrives time and again
in the company of *if, then*
The truth is, it's human nature
to plan for what we might be,
to stake our belief in *when*
and in what we can neither know
with certainty nor ever truly see

HER VICTORY

She bears down upon the page
turns her wrist to loop and curve
captures letters in her net of lead
weave heavy yet and open-knitted
like her brow in concentration
intent on closing up the cleft
between frustration and her skill
Newly licensed at age five
she stalks her quarry
comes to tears but carries on
to still the cursive *a*
subdue the cursive *g*
and claim the alphabet
her victory

taylor

INTO DAY

The river passed her,
hollow as a mokoro,
through the moon hours,
from eddy to eddy,
withheld pole, oar, paddle,
flooded the delta of sleep
with the waters of thought
didn't ask her to accept
course or current
but held her
until the hush of tall grass
slowed her bow
as dawn lit the shallows,
showed the slaty egret
in watch of silent prey,
when she could begin to see
where to step from dream's
depth out into day

TOOTH FAIRY

I kept forgetting so
you finally wrote a letter
to the tooth fairy
and at our morning hug
I snuck a bill beneath your head
under the pillow
and then too blatantly inquired
if she'd come
When the overturning at first
revealed no treasure
the effort showed
you'd left hope loose
but deliberately intact
and with discovery at last
came a new and knowing smile

SURFING LESSONS

Believe in the improbable balance
of foundation set, knees bent,
arms outstretched
Know the sea has carried more
than your concerns
Each wave new, yet one
of a continuum
of crests and troughs
Suspend your thoughts
and find the glide that comes
with wearing your skin raw,
with learning how to fall
and stand again,
to know yourself anew

BALANCE

I told her not to disembark by the bow
but to sidle up to the dock
and leave by the beam
where balance is better kept
when spread starboard to port
instead of stern to prow

Like this last year

To approach with caution
line in hand
ready to catch the cleat
at the bump of the gunwales
against wood

taylor

Ready to jump

She questioned my instruction
but I saw the moment she felt it
watched her sense
stability in the center
where gravity and buoyancy meet
She's learning now how
to read the wind and watch the sea
to shift her weight
to gauge which risks to take
and when to let go

RECALL

Now quiet,
gentle as a morning spent alone
as light moves
with the shift of the season
across the parquet floor,
ticking boxes on the calendar
marking weeks at a stretch
until the loss feels measurable
days shortened so suddenly

I don't keep a journal –
recollection, a few photos,
the only record of these years –
and hope
she'll take after my brother
who always remembers the details
I wish I could recall

FIDDLEHEAD

Furled at first
like a fiddlehead
curled and held close
to the chest
you took one chance
and a second
found with each admission
conviction grew
and you learned
to trust your path
to take the one
you felt, you knew, best
not by virtue, so-called,
by memory,
doctrine, convention,
but by trust,
to untwist worth
from action
and how you grew
as we stood witness
palms open, eyes clear,
ready to give, to share,
the fullness of you

mystic

FISHER'S POINT

The beach took her in
gave her castles and trenches
dominion over sand
offered driftwood flags
to mark her land
and a temporary stay
on subordination
the sun trimmed her in rose
and ochre pigments
and boulders took her dancing
round Fisher's point
they fed on salted air
and buttered light
while only the tide kept time

INLANDER

bound inland, will she ever learn
to be seduced by summer's air,
set early to the oar, earn
callused palm, wear dawn
across her shoulder, listen
for the break beneath her bow
and the osprey's call above
will she yearn to rise to row
ripples through the surface,
make for the horizon
and leave reason at the shore

EAST BEACH

I slept with salt on my skin,
as it should be,
wanting to ingrain in memory
the sight of you holding hands
with the child who only now is mine,
but who soon will belong to the sea,
heart forever moved
by the pull from the beach,
the cycle of waves that draws her
both nearer and farther away
You and I, we know
the strength of the tide and sun,
the tie of sand and spray
Summer, we say, is here,
where we return to ourselves,
and where, so too, will she

MUSSELED SHORE

It was only at the scene of the crime
when a sea stone,
wielded by a strong-willed girl,
met calcium bicarbonate
and mother-of-pearl,
we found we weren't the first
to imperil her.
An immature blue-shell
had come before.
A crab too new to know
had attempted a break-in,
reached into the fortification
evolution made strong.
In lieu of a feast,
the evidence showed,
he left behind his claw
in the maw of the mussel,
who closed her toothless jaws,
hid the deed within her mantle.
until her secret came to light
beside the tidal beach
under the final blow and inquest
of Nature's greater beast.

IN THE SHED

They wintered in the shed
thought, perhaps, it would make
for a safer season, a warmer home,
than a hole underground,
a nest in the eaves
In the stored trap we use
to catch plump minnows,
green crabs, thick, brown eels,
they searched out a bit of bread
The wires having trapped the scent
of the river, desiccated seaweed,
they easily found their way in
But the cage was cleverly devised,
made to engage unwitting prey
in a one-way game
And as summer turned,
she revealed an unintended catch
the sea can't claim among her own

UNSPENT

Nineteen summers unclaimed over the water
all this time
islands waiting with shores outstretched
questioning their abandonment
empty tellin shells uncollected
traps left unchecked
nineteen summers of fog over the river
of unattended sunrises
waking the horizon
and silver constellated skies
waiting for bare-skinned swimmers
nineteen summers spent sequestered inland
It took all this time
to find our way home

HUNTER

Last night
we witnessed a mystery unfold
as the lady of the cove tucked
into position, dove headfirst
from a height she knows
offers the best sight of prey

We had watched her
circle and strike before
but come up empty
This time, expectant
we waited for the victorious lift
the grappling fish in her claw
the wing beat of gray-brown
the kinked *m* of her flight
setting into the distance

But she never rose up
didn't return to the sky
though we waited, certain
somehow we had missed her
we were unprepared
for the impact of stillness
the amplitude of empty air

mystic

Now, the dawn is quiet of her call
even the gulls are gone
as if they know it's not the time
to celebrate the shell
cracked open on the weary hull
of a once-proud vessel
Only the sparrow sounds
against the current of the morning
to remind us
this is the way of the river

BEACH PLUMS

When I was young,
we ate plums at the beach
Packed them up with Saltines,
canned Tab, Coppertone
Didn't stop to think
how each piece had a price
Then, there were no stickers to peel,
branded reminders of the trip
each fruit took to reach my tongue
I never considered the maker
of the plastic bag that held them
nestled together in the cooler,
worn rubber by the roadside
shorn from the long-hauler,
pesticide that kept flesh firm,
fresh, each stone intact
They would ripen perfectly,
both soft and firm,
the way plums should be,
so juice runs down your chin,
sweet and sour at once

mystic

We'd bury the pits in the sand,
next to the cigarette butts,
cover them over and turn to the sun
So that now when my daughter
asks, Please may I have one?,
my mouth puckers
in Pavlovian response
and I think first of the pleasure
and only then of the price

HOME HOLIDAY

One of those days with nothing
on the calendar
spent at a pace
particular to summer
takes balance to get right,
between boredom and freedom,
concern over time wasted
We've forgotten how to let go,
accustomed as we are to structure,
billable hours
It's the cost of doing business,
this forgetting
Like meeting a cousin again,
the same one who shared
your secrets, the spare bed,
unscored games in the yard
Who's both familiar
and strange at once

mystic

We've been planning for weeks
to do nothing more
than follow the weather,
allow the week to remain
unaccounted for
It's a lesson in reacquaintance
with ourselves
and patience
in the collective inclination

BEST SEASON

laid down in six paths, width-wise,
white marble slabs serve as stepping stones,
reaching end over end over rich earth
to define seven rows of promise
planted two harvests deep and blooming,
the efforts of late spring:
sprawling dill, upright rosemary,
fragrant basils, crisp orange tomatoes
arriving one at a time, ready to taste,
while along the fence line,
vines of squash blossoms burst gold
and indigo petioles turn out in welcoming
the southern sun, bathing sparrows,
while the river tides run full and high
as the thunder moon comes due
and those who knew the effort
to prepare the bed, mend the gate,
agree this is the best season yet

mystic

GRANDPA'S GARDEN

She pulled back the cover of green
of pricked vine
in search of plump purple fruit

parotid glands alert
with the memory of tart juice
striking her tongue

fingers and face
stained with the pure pursuit
of pleasure

as the full buck moon
escorted the river
into the blackberry night

MYSTIC FOG

In this tangerine light,
it's hard to remember
there's ever been
a sky so encumbered
with cloud,
a cove so socked in,
I couldn't see beyond
the cover of my skin,
dare to move,
to speak aloud,
for fear of losing
my equilibrium,
for fear of falling in.

But here it is, bright again,
an improbable reawakening
brought on by rain,
by fog and by wandering.

USE THE WIND

A new storm, unexpected.
Winds collected from the bending boughs,
from around the eyes of the butterfly,
the waving grasses,
resurrected to form a new tempest,
silent but strengthening.
For just shy a moment,
the blossoms regret their audacity,
as petals strain against release,
as perigee waters rise.
But once rooted and open,
it's unlikely they'll acquiesce,
having weathered more than one cold rain,
more than one bruised sky.
It may take a turn of seasons
to reclaim their soil,
to repurpose the sun,
but it's in their nature to ascend,
to learn to use the wind,
to bloom and bloom again.

TWELVE CHANCES

Painters, dancers, scribes,
wait gibbous-eyed and wond'ring
while the tides stretch their fingers,
baptize marsh and cove
They know what the sun shares
the moon makes her own,
and they seek to follow suit,
take twelve chances,
one night of every twenty-eight,
to catch the muse in flight

mystic

FLOOD TIDE

Relief
bears the flood tide of waiting
tethered as it is to revelation
like a mooring in a nor'easter
when the line
made too short to stand
the reel of wind and water
pulls the buoy down
holds it under
until finally the air clears
the taut rope releases
and they are free again
to fully feel

HIGH WATER

Old friends meet at the shore
she, comes in from the north
he, rushes in to greet her
just the usual meeting
of wind and sea
He's eager,
but today, she won't dare him
to climb past the high-water mark
trespass beyond the sea wall
play tag on the grass
write their names in salt
across the pavement
Instead, she hushes him
directs his attention to the egret
who favors their moment of stillness
to hunt at the morning's edge

WHO WOULD BE LEGEND

Raised on folk and jazz
the sounds of rebellion
spoken in a common tongue
translated in brass and string
Unaware,
I spent my early years
among those who would be legend
learning the force of plain speech,
the influence of improvisation
Didn't need to take notes —
Those lessons fed my blood,
formed my bones
My unwitting teachers
gave me an ear for truth
a way to listen
and a reason to sing

risk

BONE, BLOOD, SKIN

We're meant to love innovation,
the constant digital wave
But give me a letter,
hand-written, stamped, and mailed
or
an illustration drawn in pen, perfect
in its imperfection
I'd like to know your mind
translated through ink and lead
Instead,
we could try the telephone,
in lieu of clipped communication,
intent abridged by screen,
by schedule,
the absence of tone,
at least there I'd learn your voice
Better yet,
I'll take you face to face
to study the upward track of surprise,
the fall of disappointment,
across the corners of your mouth,
the edges of your eyes

risk

I think I'd learn to love you, friend
There's risk, I know
We might change our minds
about each other
But I'd forgo certainty
in favor of bone and blood and skin

WHAT WOULD IT TAKE?

How will you reply when asked,
"Will you dream with me?" After all
these years of reigning in, can you
find the sense of wonder that lets
you release again, pry at your beliefs,
open to the air of possibility?
Even if only to refresh the chambers
of memory, and yet, perhaps
to exchange them for thoughts
altogether new.

What would it take
for you to dream with me?

INVITATION

From outside, I can't see in,
only a reflection
of who I think I am,
walking into an unscripted hour
Just one selected
from back-to-back engagements
out of orchestrated weeks
One stroke in time given
to draw open the door
and find you on the other side
It takes one full minute of sixty
for my eyes to adjust,
clear away distraction,
and remember why I've come
A reply to an invitation
we both extended
over the threshold of risk
with no witness
to the wish for reciprocation
except you

ESPERANZA

What fresh loss is this
friendship formed by scene
shaped by script
The air is empty now of words
the world we lived, outlived
Evidence exists by virtue
only of light and lens
and our willingness to suspend
our disbelief

BEST FRIEND

We could not have guessed
at the benefit of this acquaintance
back when we'd worn our youth
both long and through enough
to know our nature

We didn't know
how influence depends
neither on proximity nor presence
nor how it would gild the span of years
from then to now

When our willingness to suspend
the truth of days between and distance
shows how near we've always been

ALTAR OF LIVING

In my peripheral vision,
chestnut turns temple-white,
transformed as an offering
on the altar of living
It occurs at the same time
as sight shifting, as if
to show near-term as only
part of the picture
A new kind of vision
that permits less focus
on the ascender
or tail of the letter
and more on the spirit
of its stroke
I see concerns of the moment,
heavy though they are,
are but stones for building
the monument of life
and the same matter
we'll later invoke
to inscribe our closing words

BARTON SPRINGS

Action is perhaps the only cure
for uncertainty
Its remedy deep and sure enough
to hold the interest and resolve
of late companions
who test its edge
pose the question of risk,
reward, who at first
take care, practice caution
but having waited,
already have their answer

THE RECORD

A poor measure of years, productivity
At the end, I shouldn't wish a list,
but rather, a measure of love,
to stand for newly open space, quiet air
Even so, I'm inclined to assess my worth
through yield, equate consequence
with throughput, attend to what's ahead
and what's behind, while
all the time, the record of regard
is mine alone to make
and the effect of loving, endless

AIRBNB

Days soft in direction
pillowed on either end
with hazy sleep
and between
the bright snap of sheets
coffee darkly brewed
and the cleanse of sea
a chance to keep
the unfamiliar close
bend routine
and walk in step
let words give shape
appoint momentum
with emptied bottles
shared plates
for a change
spend entire skies
awake to late dreams

PARALLEL

open on two friends
reconnected
recalling
how paths may run
parallel and rejoin
how to walk over
the crushed stone
of misunderstanding
without tripping
without failing
instead
choosing to hold up
hold on
aware of now
and what's ahead
of how and where
the trail will rise
even if they take it
apart

ACCELERATION

Each introduction
a nodal point in learning,
a new genius to be understood,
heard out, hand shaken,
part of the centrifuge
of acceleration
gathering up ideas, sorting
a shoebox of experiences,
to weigh against our own,
spin down and reflect, adjust, distill
into direction that's still a gamble,
still a bet, an educated guess
But what isn't? I'd rather risk
a little pride, a little pragmatism,
to know what it is
to attempt a new invention
watch how curiosity comes to light
from the most ordinary of concerns
and answers derive from figures no more
or less than us together
and a willingness to question
if the current solution is best
or if discovery lies just ahead

ENTREPRENEUR

Days newly spent consumed by acronyms,
puzzling out the applied meaning
behind accepted initialisms
and making up our own for fun
and the practice of standing at the helm
We write the scene: midday,
two women in a living room,
face to face, vision to vision,
working through the permutations
of models and innovation,
trying to guess at what we don't know
and can't possibly predict
in the face of IoT, the singularity,
VUI, UI/UX
How to differentiate, make space
for our new sons, TAM, SAM, SOM
Who knew we'd be mothers again?
Flipping through the pages of our handbook
to see if our little one
is meeting the milestones for growth

risk

This time,
screen time a predictor of health,
and play dates with mentors, investors,
advisors who might intersect,
click with our problem-solution,
say "I do" to traction, team, call-to-action
I'm learning perhaps art and business
aren't mutually exclusive (herewith, proof),
and MRR but one axis of success
when the quest requires creation as evidence
and yields a network of new thought

SILENT MEANING

Silence slips between thoughts,
lifts lip and tongue for air
to retreat and escape
They sense
there's enough in what's between,
left ahead,
for meaning to remain clear
in the absence of speech
Moments of breath and belief
there's more in what's missing
than might ever be said

BETWEEN

In the hollows between hello
a smoke-blue cascade falls
stage-by-stage
over the warm stones of routine
tries the edge
to test how far it can flow
above the banks of convention
and courses on
fed by a wellspring below
that both conceals and renews
its source

TO REST

For just a moment,
I want to surrender.
(Is this familiar?)
Give up
what I've made, set in motion.
Divest of preference, desire.
For a time without interest.
(Have you felt this?)
Allow voice and muscle to rest,
engage only for survival.
To step back and merely watch.
Like when we were kids,
when growth was inevitable.
(Do you remember?)
When instinct instructed
when to run for safety,
run for your life,
and even when to stand in place.

CLIMB ON

Up the pitch,
she led by increments,
setting anchors en route,
singular points secured
against a fall
Each move a blend
of instinct, training,
guesswork, a decade
of conditioning
With every hitch
a new consideration,
problem to be solved
On the face of it,
from a distance,
the path evident,
but up close, a series
of moves that try
skill, breath, strength,
that rely on belay
and a basis of trust

THE RUNNER

Thigh and calf
cast by a lover of length,
of long, thin limbs,
and of youth,
so that even in mid-life,
she won't bear the signs of age,
save for in her eyes,
the corners of her mouth,
which reveal her truth
Trunk as lean and strong
as when she ran the woods,
and mind as keen, still racing,
meeting option's pace
With will her only weight,
and none of child, nor of place,
she'll run on, stretch long
beyond root and branch and stone,
build muscle over bone
and a mind to match
her body's strength

PAUSE

They pause at each
new point of interest;
assess its effect
Attempt to record
from this vantage
what's easy to forget
up close
When they can't hold,
contact, can't address
what they sense
Independent, separate, yet
part of one experience

PROMISE

For later, she saved promise, folded
into seemingly impossible size, tucked
hope into the coin pocket where she kept
the shards of a paper heart, the sharp
slivers from the center, trimmed to shape
the globe just right, so that opening
felt like flight, wings worth the effort,
the awkward ache of blade outgrown,
saved with the ephemera of love set free

risk

WORTH KEEPING

This collection of stones I've saved
from Kala Patthar, Koh Samui,
Playa Flamingo, Dragon's Back
gathered together here by my bedside
I don't know which is from where
but they help me recall the life I've led

The full moon dawning over East Beach,
over the Osa Peninsula, over the Okavango
each round rock a recollection
worn of rough edges
burnished smooth through time

I've seen enough to know
that while the earth below
is made entirely of minerals
each sweet stone is worth keeping
especially when the memory is new

CALL & RESPONSE

They took turns
trading leather-wrapped hammer,
inlaid with bone,
for clean-honed chisel,
bright still from stone and oil
Balanced handle, hand exposed,
under coiled muscle, forged steel,
ready to embrace the force
of instinct and will
to shape the space between them
Through question and answer,
beats of call and response,
they found in trust the greater tool
to reveal what they could become

SECOND ACT

Now closing in on mid-century,
the center point of life, if I'm lucky,
I've seen choice and fate play out,
twin children of mortality,
watched them fight and make up
As mother to one, subject to the other,
I'm not entitled to regret
but employ doubt to wonder
how to use this suffrage anew,
take each child's hand in mine,
affect change to best effect,
and together stage the second act

DC TO PENN

On the 178 from DC to Penn
they made a trade between stations
learned the rate of conversion
between time and acquaintance
with nothing to gain
save for the line of rail ahead
and through an ancient exchange
two unfamiliar friends
found new destinations

HALF-LIFE

In carbon dating, the ratio of C to N
tells time of death, even years in
Like the way love appears stable
from the outside
but breaks down over time –
one part habit, one part heart –
how unattended, it devolves
into a substance unfamiliar
fatal, even, to its own survival

You won't find it on the periodic table,
but I could swear it has atomic weight
Like matter, it's not created or destroyed
but changes shape
Perhaps, beyond words,
we simply haven't yet devised
the tools to measure and record it
but most of us have observed
the half-life of love

LOVE, UNDONE

We're told we shouldn't take offense
at the glass left by the sink,
laundry untouched,
bed unmade with the plans
for anything more than the status quo
Though by now we know by heart
each omission as theft,
left to amount to love undone

REASON & REPAIR

With practice,
I've learned to look away
from what we've resolved
In the same way we come
to overlook the rutted path
that leads to the familiar door
with the sticky lock,
stacks of unopened mail,
the shaky handrail on the stair
Mostly, I forget,
until acceptance turns to attention,
a momentary upset in routine,
and the need to envision a before
or since or now
that didn't allow for restitution
Where would we be, then?
Such a mix of tenses to address
in the possibilities of yesterday
and a reminder of the shifting nature
of love's reason and repair

CHRISTIA MADACSI HOFFMAN is a native of Mystic, Connecticut, and a longtime resident of Austin, Texas. A writer by nature and trade, her poetry collections are curated from a daily poetry practice she began in 2013. Hoffman's first collection of poems, *Intent*, was published in 2017; this is her second collection of poetry.

Made in the USA
Columbia, SC
25 September 2022

67746441R00112